A Note From Rick Renner

I am on a personal quest to see a "revival of the Bible" so people can establish their lives on a firm foundation that will stand strong and endure the test as end-time storm winds begin to intensify.

In order to experience a revival of the Bible in your personal life, it is important to take time each day to read, receive, and apply its truths to your life. James tells us that if we will continue in the perfect law of liberty — refusing to be forgetful hearers, but determined to be doers — we will be blessed in our ways. As you watch or listen to the programs in this series and work through this corresponding study guide, I trust you will search the Scriptures and allow the Holy Spirit to help you hear something new from God's Word that applies specifically to your life. I encourage you to be a doer of the Word He reveals to you. Whatever the cost, I assure you — it will be worth it.

> Thy words were found, and I did eat them;
> and thy word was unto me the joy and rejoicing of mine heart:
> for I am called by thy name, O Lord God of hosts.
> — Jeremiah 15:16

Your brother and friend in Jesus Christ,

Rick Renner

Unless otherwise indicated, all scripture quotations are taken from the *King James Version* of the Bible.

Overcoming Surprise Attacks in Your Life

Copyright © 2018 by Rick Renner
1814 W. Tacoma St.
Broken Arrow, OK 74012-1406

Published by Rick Renner Ministries
www.renner.org

ISBN 13: 978-1-6803-1592-9

ISBN 13 eBook: 978-1-6803-1630-8

How To Use This Study Guide

This four-lesson study guide corresponds to *"Overcoming Surprise Attacks in Your Life" with Rick Renner* (Renner TV). Each lesson covers a topic that is addressed during the program series, with questions and references supplied to draw you deeper into your own private study of the Scriptures on this subject.

To derive the most benefit from this study guide, consider the following:

First, watch or listen to the program prior to working through the corresponding lesson in this guide. (Programs can also be viewed at **renner.org** by clicking on the Media/Archives links or on our Renner Ministries YouTube channel.)

Second, take the time to look up the scriptures included in each lesson. Prayerfully consider their application to your own life.

Third, use a journal or notebook to make note of your answers to each lesson's Study Questions and Practical Application challenges.

Fourth, invest specific time in prayer and in the Word of God to consult with the Holy Spirit. Write down the scriptures or insights He reveals to you.

Finally, take action! Whatever the Lord tells you to do according to His Word, do it.

For added insights on this subject, it is recommended that you obtain Rick Renner's book *Life in the Combat Zone*. You may also select from Rick's other available resources by placing your order at **renner.org** or by calling 1-800-742-5593.

TOPIC

You Can Overcome Any Circumstance

SCRIPTURES

1. **1 Thessalonians 2:17, 18** — But we, brethren, being taken from you for a short time in presence, not in heart, endeavoured the more abundantly to see your face with great desire. Wherefore we would have come unto you, even I, Paul, once and again; but Satan hindered us.

2. **Romans 8:28** — And we know that all things work together for good to them that love God, to them who are the called according to his purpose.

3. **Romans 8:37** — Nay, in all these things we are more than conquerors through him that loved us.

GREEK WORDS

1. "Satan" — **Σατανᾶς** (*satanas*): one who hates, accuses, slanders, or conspires against

2. "hindered" — **ἐγκόπτω** (*egkopto*): to cut in on; to elbow out of the way; to block a road; to create an impasse; a disruption

3. "all things" — **πάντα** (*panta*): everything; nothing excluded

4. "work together" — **συνεργέω** (*sunergeo*): to cooperate; to work together; to assist

SYNOPSIS

The four lessons in this study of *Overcoming Surprise Attacks in Your Life* will emphasize the following topics:

1. You Can Overcome Any Circumstance
2. Fighting 'Wild Beasts' That Attack Your Life
3. Taking Authority Over Spiritual Turbulence
4. Your Best Defense Against an Attack

The emphasis of this lesson:

If you will stay in faith, God will cause all things to work together for your good (Romans 8:28).

No matter what the devil may toss in your path to prevent you from reaching your destination, if you will stay in faith, God will get involved to remove the impasse and turn that surprise attack into a setup for your success!

At the time when the first church was established in the city of Aphrodisias — a historic city in western Turkey dedicated to the goddess Aphrodite — as many as 30,000 spectators would gather to watch assorted fights and competitive games. The activities would include wild-animal fights, chariot races, and gladiator contests where believers were sometimes thrust into the arena to die at the hands of gladiators. Among these events were the popular foot races. In fact, these races were so popular that the apostle Paul often drew illustrations from the foot races in the stadiums to make different points as he taught.

An example of one such illustration is found in First Thessalonians 2:17 and 18, where Paul stated, "But we, brethren, being taken from you for a short time in presence, not in heart, endeavoured the more abundantly to see your face with great desire. Wherefore we would have come unto you, even I, Paul, once and again; but Satan hindered us."

The word "hindered" in this passage is the Greek word *egkopto*, which presents a picture of *one runner giving the race his best efforts until a competing runner unexpectedly thrusts an elbow into his side to cut in front of him or to push or elbow him out of the race.* By using this example, Paul was telling the Thessalonians: *"I really wanted to come to you, and I made several attempts. But even I, Paul, got elbowed off the path along the way by Satan on multiple occasions with a surprise attack of trouble on the way."*

The Greek word *satanas* is not so much the name of the devil as it is the description of the activity Satan uses to hinder us. The word *satanas* means *one who hates us; one who accuses, slanders, and conspires against to disrupt us.*

Have you ever thought you were right in the middle of God's will, but suddenly you experienced a disruption that hindered you? You can't always know why. But one thing is certain: The devil doesn't want you to arrive at God's destination for your life — because if you do, the enemy knows that the power of God will be released and His divine will engaged. Satan will therefore toss an impasse in your path or create a disruption to stop you.

If you give up and throw in the towel because you experience too much opposition, you're done. You must be willing to say, *No! I'm not stopping! I will press forward for my marriage and for my children!* If you'll stay in faith, you will be the one who will cut in and elbow the devil out! You will be one who remains in the will of God, staying right where He wants you to be.

But you must be tenacious. The Bible makes it very clear that you do indeed have an adversary.

Paul had a lot of disruptions (*see* 2 Corinthians 11:22-27), but he stayed in faith.

I can give the same testimony from my own life. Denise and I have experienced many attacks over the years while we were doing what God called us to do. But rather than faint in the day of adversity, we stayed in faith. God is so gracious to those whom He calls. He makes all that the devil used to conspire against us — all those events that at the time seemed so tragic — to work together for our good (*see* Romans 8:28). He actually turned those past negative experiences around and caused them to advance us to a new level!

None of Satan's strategies to destroy the Church has ever succeeded. By studying Church history, it becomes evident very quickly that each attack the enemy has waged against the Church has ultimately helped to further the cause of Jesus Christ. Two thousand years of experience emphatically tell us that the devil has absolutely no winning strategies. He simply does not know how to win!

— *Excerpt from* Dressed To Kill, *page 118*

I can't begin to count the times in our own ministry when the devil has severely attacked and pounded us, trying to drive us back and convince us to give up territory. But we made the decision that we weren't budging and we were *not* going to flinch.

When you refuse to faint in the day of adversity, God will cause you to be more than a conqueror! (*see* Romans 8:37). In Christ Jesus, you are an overwhelming, walloping force through the One who loved us and washed us from our sins in His own blood (*see* Revelation 1:5). Even if the devil has conspired against you, slandering you to prevent you from reaching your point of destination, he is the one who is the ultimate loser. When God jumps in, the devil cannot win! God will make all things work together *for* you as He works together *with* you to help you reach your divinely ordained destination.

STUDY QUESTIONS

**Study to shew thyself approved unto God,
a workman that needeth not to be ashamed,
rightly dividing the word of truth.
— 2 Timothy 2:15**

1. How does Satan typically hinder people from reaching their God-ordained destination? In what ways has he hindered you?
2. What is the primary response you must consistently walk in to ensure that God will get involved to turn a situation around for you after the devil tries to cut in and elbow you off course? How have you responded in the past when surprise attacks struck your life?
3. What is the scriptural basis for your confidence that you can emerge victorious from any attack of the devil?
4. Other than the apostle Paul, cite three scriptural accounts of people who overcame surprise or severe attacks of the devil.

PRACTICAL APPLICATION

**But be ye doers of the word, and not hearers only,
deceiving your own selves.
—James 1:22**

1. You may have experienced a surprise attack that didn't seem to end well for you. In retrospect, consider the ways God actually got involved to lessen the severity of what Satan intended to do to destroy you. In the future, how can you better cooperate with divine intervention in your life?

2. A strong or courageous spirit can sustain you in times of difficulty (*see* Proverbs 18:14). Write down the measures you are taking on a daily basis to strengthen your spirit and cultivate endurance so a "surprise attack" won't catch you unprepared to stand strong.

LESSON 2

TOPIC

Fighting Wild Beasts That Attack Your Life

SCRIPTURES

1. **1 Corinthians 15:32** — If after the manner of men I have fought with beasts at Ephesus, what advantageth it me, if the dead rise not? let us eat and drink; for to morrow we die.

2. **Romans 8:28** — And we know that all things work together for good to them that love God, to them who are the called according to his purpose.

3. **2 Timothy 2:9** — Wherein I suffer trouble, as an evil doer, even unto bonds; but the word of God is not bound.

4. **James 1:17** — Every good gift and every perfect gift is from above, and cometh down from the Father of lights, with whom is no variableness, neither shadow of turning.

GREEK WORDS

1. "I have fought with beasts" — **θηριομαχέω** (*theriomacheo*)
   θηρίον (*therion*): to fight a wild beast; to fight a dangerous animal; to fight a vicious killer
   μάχομαι (*machomai*): I fight, usually with weapons
2. "all things" — **πάντα** (*panta*): everything; nothing excluded
3. "work together" — **συνεργέω** (*sunergeo*): to cooperate; to work together; to assist
4. "bound" — **δέω** (*deo*): bound; tied up; restricted; imprisoned
5. "found" — **εὑρίσκω** (*heurisko*): I find or discover; a "eureka" moment

SYNOPSIS

In the great stadium located in ancient Ephesus, competitive games and fights would be conducted in the morning. Spectators would gather by the thousands to watch humans use weapons to fight all kinds of wild, ferocious man-killing beasts. In this very arena, the apostle Paul tells us in First Corinthians 15:32 that he had fought wild beasts in Ephesus.

Some have thought Paul said he fought wild beasts as an allegorical illustration. But to say this to people who daily faced the threat of being thrown into the arena and torn apart by vicious animals as sport would be thoroughly inappropriate. No, Paul was writing to people who knew of such dangers, and he was more than likely letting them know that he, too, literally fought wild beasts with weapons in the arena of Ephesus and survived to tell about it.

The devil is very serious about victimizing you. You, too, may feel as though you are fighting wild beasts. It might be a situation that's trying to maul you and take you down. But just like those beasts couldn't take Paul down because of the Greater One in him, you can release the power of God in your life to conquer and vanquish every foe.

The emphasis of this lesson:

God will get involved to help you overcome demonic attacks strategized against you.

When Paul was imprisoned in Rome, he wrote his second epistle to Timothy. In Second Timothy 2:9, Paul wrote that although he was suffering trouble unto bonds, the Word of God was not bound, restricted, or imprisoned.

Satan had conspired to put Paul out of commission. But the devil is incapable of winning, and he always overplays his hand. The enemy made a tragic miscalculation that backfired because Paul refused to give up, lose heart, or discard his faith. God Himself got involved and set up Paul to use his stationary time in prison as a steppingstone from which he could propel the Gospel of Jesus Christ around the world. Although Paul could not go where he wanted to go, he picked up parchment and pen to write letters, declaring the Word of God was not bound, even though *he* was. And through his many handwritten letters that were widely circulated and reproduced, Paul's ministry has continued to produce fruit for 2,000 years!

In Acts 18, we see another instance of God turning a tragic situation into a magnificent moment that furthered His plan. Claudius, the emperor of Rome, became so upset about the contention between believing and the non-believing Jews that he kicked out *all* the Jews from the city of Rome. Among them were a husband and wife named Aquila and Priscilla. This couple had a successful business, friends, and an established social network in the city. But in one irreversible decision, they were suddenly evicted from Rome, along with every other Jew in the city. Suddenly their entire lives were dismantled. Everything was gone in an attack they never could have anticipated.

Aquila and Priscilla decided to board a boat that took them eastward and disembark at the port on the western side of Greece near the city of Corinth. When they got off the boat, they didn't know what they would do. Still reeling from the unexpected attack, Aquila and Priscilla headed toward Corinth, where they experienced something amazing. Acts 18:1 and 2 relates that strategic moment: "After these things Paul departed from Athens, and came to Corinth. And found a certain Jew named Aquila, born in Pontus, lately come from Italy, with his wife Priscilla; (because that Claudius had commanded all Jews to depart from Rome:) and came unto them."

At the most desperate point when all seemed lost for Aquila and Priscilla, God got involved to make all things work together for good. Walking into Corinth, "Paul *found* them" (v. 2). The couple and the apostle literally bumped into each other as they all made their way into the unfamiliar pagan city. The surprise attack that had begun as a tragedy for Aquila and Priscilla ultimately resulted in becoming one of their greatest blessings. Everything turned because God intervened and connected them to Paul.

As a result of that divine connection, Aquila and Priscilla accomplished things for God's Kingdom they had never dreamed of accomplishing in their wildest imagination. They helped Paul start the church of Corinth and, later, the church of Ephesus. Their relationship with the apostle literally launched them into their greatest phase of ministry. The devil intended to use that eviction from their home in Rome to destroy them. But God made it a steppingstone to send them where they would not even know how to go by themselves.

Just as God turned around that crisis for the good of Aquila and Priscilla, He's going to do the same for you concerning the challenges you face in life.

STUDY QUESTIONS

> **Study to shew thyself approved unto God,**
> **a workman that needeth not to be ashamed,**
> **rightly dividing the word of truth.**
> **— 2 Timothy 2:15**

1. Paul endured many attacks, yet he survived to testify that God delivered him from them all. Cite several other Bible accounts that are examples of God turning what the enemy meant for evil into good in the lives of those who held onto their faith.

2. In Second Corinthians 11:23-28, Paul described a series of dangers he encountered that were not listed in the book of Acts. What

were the circumstances of those attacks, and how did Paul emerge from them?

3. The Bible assures us: "And we know that all things work together for good to them that love God, to them who are the called according to his purpose" (Romans 8:28). It emphatically does *not* say that God makes everything happen. God never sends evil. We know that every good and perfect gift is from above, as it says in James 1:17. If something comes from God, it's good. If it comes from the devil, it is bad, evil, destructive, and tragic. What are some of the ways God has turned negative events that have happened in your life to your good? Have you held on to your faith and confident expectation that you *will see* the goodness of the Lord in the land of the living (*see* Psalm 27:13)?

PRACTICAL APPLICATION

> **But be ye doers of the word, and not hearers only,**
> **deceiving your own selves.**
> **— James 1:22**

1. A closed door does not mean failure — even if it slams shut in your face. God may be opening the largest door that's ever been available to you. If you will stay in place and refuse to budge or surrender any territory, no matter what's happening, God will respond to your faith, get involved, and turn those events to assist His plan for your life. God will take the most minuscule detail and make it work together for your benefit.

2. If you are facing an irreversible situation that looks as though you've lost everything, fasten your expectation on God and begin to thank Him for the "Eureka!" moment coming your way — because a divinely orchestrated opportunity is about to find you!

TOPIC

Taking Authority Over Spiritual Turbulence

SCRIPTURES

Mark 4:35-41 — And the same day, when the even was come, he saith unto them, Let us pass over unto the other side. And when they had sent away the multitude, they took him even as he was in the ship. And there were also with him other little ships. And there arose a great storm of wind, and the waves beat into the ship, so that it was now full. And he was in the hinder part of the ship, asleep on a pillow: and they awake him, and say unto him, Master, carest thou not that we perish? And he arose, and rebuked the wind, and said unto the sea, Peace, be still. And the wind ceased, and there was a great calm. And he said unto them, Why are ye so fearful? how is it that ye have no faith? And they feared exceedingly, and said one to another, What manner of man is this, that even the wind and the sea obey him?

GREEK WORDS

1. "there arose" — γίνομαι (*ginomai*): to take by surprise; to take off-guard; not anticipated

2. "great" — μεγάλη (*megale*): great; enormous

3. "storm" — λαῖλαψ (*lailaps*): atmospheric turbulence

4. "waves" — κύματα (*kumata*): billowing waves; one wave after another; a succession of waves

5. "beat into" — ἐπιβάλλω (*epiballo*): The picture of picking up and throwing; to throw over; to throw against

6. "Lord" — Κύριε (*Kurie*): a sovereign; sovereignty

7. "Teacher" — Διδάσκαλε (*Didaskale*): a masterful teacher; a rabbi; one who teachers

8. "Master" — Ἐπιστάτα (*Epistata*): a master; a commander

9. "carest" — μέλει (*melei*): to worry; to feel anxiety; to be concerned

10. "perish" — ἀπόλλυμι (*apollumi*): to undo; to perish; to destroy

11. "rebuked" — ἐπιτιμάω (*epitimao*): to speak dishonorably to someone; to sternly speak against; to chide; to rebuke

12. "wind" — ἀνέμου (*anemou*): a storm-like force

13. "peace be still" — φιμόω (*phimoo*): to be muzzled; to be silent; to be still

14. "calm" — γαλήνη (*galena*): calm; tranquility; serene

15. "fearful" — δειλός (*deilos*): cowards; timidity; no gumption

16. "obey" — ὑπακούω (*hupakouo*): to submit and explicitly obey; to fall in line when an order is given

SYNOPSIS

The emphasis of this lesson is twofold:

1. If you stay in faith, your place of suffering will actually become your cave of revelation as Jesus steps in to bring you fresh revelation of who He is to you in that situation.

2. When you take authority over the invisible turbulence and unseen winds, what you do see will settle down and come into line.

The devil tries to attack when you're on the way to do the will of God. Maybe you were on the way to fulfill your dream. And then something happened. You were disrupted. You lost your job. Your finances got messed up. Something happened in a relationship — something totally unanticipated.

That's what happened to the apostle John. He was living in Ephesus, doing everything God wanted him to do. But one day there was a knock on his door. Soldiers came to arrest him by the command of the Emperor Domitian. John was brought to trial for his faith. Some historical writers say he was then thrown into a vat of boiling oil — but he emerged *unscathed*.

When that failed to kill the apostle as Domitian intended, John was banished to the barren, desolate prison island of Patmos, where he lived in a cave. Who would have ever thought that kind of suffering would be inflicted upon an elderly man who just loved people? But

Jesus stepped into that cave on Patmos with John, and John received a brand-new revelation of the exalted Jesus.

The devil will be sorry that he ever attacked you — because when you're attacked and you hold fast to your faith in God, that place of attack usually becomes a place of divine revelation. If you're hit with sickness and steadfastly believe God for your healing, that's when you gain new revelation that Jesus is the Healer. If your finances come under assault, the devil thinks he's going to take you down.

But if you hold fast by faith to God's promises, that attack becomes your cave where you meet *Jehovah Jireh* — the God who provides. You gain a revelation of God's supernatural provision. Whatever the devil has been doing to you, he will regret it because God will step into that situation with you and reveal Himself.

Vicious attacks usually come at critical points when something important is about to occur. Each one is a clear attempt to thwart the plan of God.

That's what the devil does. He tries to create an impasse to block you. Anytime you're on the front lines of battle and doing something significant for the Kingdom of God, the enemy's attack against your life will probably escalate.

Even Jesus came under an unexpected attack. Before He was preparing to cast a legion of demons out of the demoniac of Gadara, a violent and destructive storm came to kill and destroy. The devil didn't want Jesus in the country of the Gadarenes.

This was a preemptive strike to prevent the power of God from being released, not only to deliver that man but also to deliver that entire region, held captive because of what controlled him. The fact that this attack came just as Jesus was on the brink of a major miracle is not uncommon. This is normally when attacks occur. Therefore, we must mentally and spiritually prepare ourselves to deal with demonic attacks. We're to put on the whole armor of God and take authority over the wind and the waves that come against our lives, our families, our businesses, or our bodies, just like Jesus took authority over the turbulent wind and the waves that came against Him. (*See Dressed To Kill*, page 45.)

When turbulence rose up in opposition to Jesus as He was on His way to release a mighty breakthrough in Gadara, Jesus demonstrated how we are to respond to a surprise attack and emerge victorious every time.

How do *you* respond to a surprise attack?

- Remember the word of the Lord about your assignment ("Let us pass to the other side").
- Stay in faith, trust God, and refuse to quit. The attack that surprised you is no surprise to Him.
- Take authority and deal with the invisible realm; then take care of the natural realm.
- Receive fresh revelation of who Jesus is as He steps in to help you handle the storm.

STUDY QUESTIONS

**Study to shew thyself approved unto God,
a workman that needeth not to be ashamed,
rightly dividing the word of truth.
— 2 Timothy 2:15**

1. What is the specific "word of the Lord" that Satan is challenging in your life? How does recalling that word enable you to "wage a good warfare" as Paul instructed us to do in First Timothy 1:18?
2. How has the Lord revealed Himself to you in a fresh way recently? What word did He reveal to your heart that His Spirit confirmed in your circumstances? What is the scriptural foundation of that revelation? How has that revelation changed you?
3. The storms of life come to everyone. In the last storm you passed through, were you resting or fitfully bailing water? What scriptures are you pouring into your heart now so that when you are pressed on every side again, the strength and courage those scriptures produce will pour out of you?

PRACTICAL APPLICATION

**But be ye doers of the word, and not hearers only,
deceiving your own selves.
— James 1:22**

1. Deal with the source, not the symptoms. Speak to the unseen wind at work behind the waves billowing in your life. When you address the invisible, the visible will be easier to handle.

2. "As He is, so are we in this world" (1 John 4:17). Just as Jesus slept without anxious fear because he knew He was going to the other side, exercise your faith in God's promise to you by choosing rest instead of giving place to agitated thoughts. Then exercise your authority in Christ to enforce the peace of God in the atmosphere around you. It is the authority within your spirit that causes the devil to obey.

3. Read Ephesians 6. Fortify your own conviction of what you look like to the devil: fully clothed in the armor of God and well-trained in how to wield each piece of weaponry.

LESSON 4

TOPIC

Your Best Defense Against an Attack

SCRIPTURES

Acts 19:23, 24 — And the same time there arose no small stir about that way. For a certain man named Demetrius, a silversmith, which made silver shrines for Diana, brought no small gain unto the craftsmen.

GREEK WORDS

1. "stir" — τάραχος (*tarachos*): trouble; uproar; disturbance
2. "persuaded" — πείθω (*peitho*): persuasion; one who is convinced, coaxed, or swayed from one opinion to another, a persuasion that

leads to conviction and belief; absolute confidence; convinced to the core; rock-solid certainty

3. "turned away" — μεθίστημι (*methistimi*): to change one's position; to pervert

4. "danger" — κίνδυνος (*kindunos*): danger, peril, risk

5. "set at nought" — ἀπελεγμός (*apelegmos*): exposure; examination; rejection after examination

6. "magnificence" — μεγαλειότης (*megaleiotes*): majesty; splendor; glory; magnificence

7. "destroyed" — καθαιρέω (*kathareo*): pulled down; torn down; destroyed; dismantled; destroyed with nothing left standing

8. "wrath" — θυμός (*thumos*): outburst of passion; uncontrolled rage, anger, or wrath

9. "confusion" — σύγχυσις (*sunchusis*): confused emotions; mixed-up passions; a volatile mess

10. "having caught" — συναρπάζω (*sunarpadzo*): caught; seize, snatch, or drag

11. "companions in travel" — συνέκδημος (*sunekdemos*): fellow travelers; traveling associates

12. "one accord" — ὁμοθυμαδόν (*homothumadon*): an unplanned, spontaneous eruption at one precise moment

13. "would" — βούλομαι (*boulomai*): intending, resolving, determining, or planning

14. "suffered him" — ἐάω (*eao*): to leave alone; to let one make a bad mistake; misgivings

15. "men of Asia" — Ἀσιάρχης (*Asiarches*): Asiarch, one of ten leading men in Asia connected with the worship of the emperor in the Roman province of Asia

16. "friends" — φίλος (*philos*): friend with whom one has a friendly relationship; a relationship from which two or more have derived mutual value

17. "desiring" — παρακαλέω (*parakaleo*): begging; pleading; counseling; praying; even to provide legal counsel

18. "town clerk" — γραμματεύς (*grammateus*): city administrator; one of the highest officials in the city of Ephesus

19. "robbers of churches" — ἱερόσυλος (*hierosulos*): robbers of temples; plunderers of temples; sacrilegious
20. "blasphemers" — βλασφημέω (*blasphemeo*): to speak crudely, rudely, disrespectfully, or discourteously
21. "cause" — αἴτιος (*aitios*): no cause; no crime; no actionable offense
22. "dismissed" — ἀπολύω (*apoluo*): to undo, unloose, unravel, dismiss, or release

SYNOPSIS

The emphasis of this lesson:

A life of personal consecration is your best defense against a demonic attack.

When the apostle Paul came into Ephesus with Aquila and Priscilla and they began to preach, there was a great revival. The Church was established with demonstrations of signs and wonders. Pagans were attracted from all over the city. And when they heard the message of Jesus Christ, Acts 19 says they began to repent of their wicked deeds and their curious arts, which involved the worship of idols.

When the people began to turn from their idols, the idolmakers became furious because it affected their business. Thousands of idolmakers met in the Theater of Ephesus to revolt against the preaching of the Gospel. The Bible tells us that they raised their voices in menacing shouts for the span of two hours. Yet that great tumult was ultimately nothing more than the dying screams of a religion being slain by the preaching of the Gospel.

The revolt on that day took the apostle Paul and his friends completely off guard. It was a surprise — nearly fatal — attack they never anticipated. After Demetrius inflamed the crowd with accusations against Paul, the city administrator (who was the highest ranking local official in the city of Ephesus) rose to Paul's defense and said: "Ye men of Ephesus, what man is there that knoweth not how that the city of Ephesus is a worshipper of the great goddess Artemis? Seeing then that these things cannot be spoken against or questioned, ye ought to be quiet, and do nothing rashly."

Paul had not been disrespectful toward their false religion. He had been very intellectual in his approach and simply preached the truth of the Gospel with the power of God evident. The city administrator went on to tell the crowd of idolmakers that if they had any legal claim, the deputies could deal with it. But as it stood, the instigators were the ones in danger of being called into question by the authorities for their riotous demonstration, which was groundless and incited without cause.

Paul had not done anything wrong — no crime, no offense. There was nothing the apostle had done for them to stir up that big disturbance. So in verse 41, it says, "When he had thus spoken, the city administrator dismissed the assembly." The word "dismissed" means *to unloose, undo, unravel, dismiss, and to release.* He basically said, *"There's nothing in these men that can be attacked. They've done nothing wrong. We may not like their message or its effect on our economy, but there's nothing in them that we can accuse on a personal level, so be quiet and leave."* That was it.

Demon spirits have absolutely no power to bring about destruction unless they can find an open door. If they locate such an entrance into the mind and practices of a person, from that position they begin to launch their attacks against a person's life. The tendency of flesh has always been to blame personal failure on someone else or on some external circumstance that was beyond their goal. Shifting blame is as old as the Garden of Eden. But you cannot blame your failure on anyone else. You can't even blame your failure on a demonic attack.

In order for a demonic attack to work, *you had to cooperate in some way either through ignorance, through deliberate cooperation, or through negligence by refusing to deal with some private area of your life that you knew was wrong and you needed to fix.* You may say the devil is attacking your money, but if you fail to balance your checkbook or are irresponsible in paying your bills, you're the one who opened the door for him to enter and steal. You may say the enemy is attempting to afflict you with sickness. But if you abused your body by eating wrong, overworking, and pushing your body beyond its capabilities, you opened the door for your body to be attacked.

You can cry that your marriage is under assault. But if you often speak harshly to your spouse, never spend any time with him or her, and have not made your marriage a priority, you have thrown open the door for the enemy to come in and destroy your marriage. (See *Dressed to Kill* by Rick Renner, pages 42-50).

The majority of attacks and tragedies could be avoided. They occur because of doors left open to the enemy through anger, bitterness, wrath, or slothfulness. Sneak attacks are real, but demon spirits cannot destroy a person unless there is already an area in his or her life they can grab hold of and twist to that person's destruction.

There were no such areas in the life of the apostle Paul — nothing that the devil could use to destroy him. Therefore, Paul's personal consecration to the Lord was his greatest defense against the enemy. Although Paul was outwardly buffeted, he was never attacked to the point of personal failure. He lived a crucified life. He was dead to sin. Nothing in him cooperated with the devil's temptations and devices. Paul's personal consecration paralyzed the devil's ability to make him fail.

So we can conclude from a study of Paul's life that it's very difficult — if not entirely impossible — for the devil to completely destroy a person who lives a sanctified and consecrated life. Most attacks would be totally avoided if sin, bad behavior, and wrong attitudes were not permitted to have a place in a believer's life.

Your personal consecration is your best defense.

STUDY QUESTIONS

**Study to shew thyself approved unto God,
a workman that needeth not to be ashamed,
rightly dividing the word of truth.
— 2 Timothy 2:15**

1. In the hour of His greatest attack, Jesus said in John 14:30, "The prince of this world cometh, and hath nothing in me." You can be certain the enemy is coming to find something to exploit in your life. Has the Holy Spirit been dealing with you to change your ways in certain areas? Now is a good time to remove the enemy's legal claims against you to make sure your own life can stand as a shield of defense in that day when you're hit with a surprise attack.

2. If you undergo one attack after another, barely able to catch your breath, take an honest look at your life. Are you living in such a way that the devil has nothing to grab hold of to use against you?

PRACTICAL APPLICATION

> **But be ye doers of the word, and not hearers only,**
> **deceiving your own selves.**
> **—James 1:22**

1. When the enemy brings a charge against you, pointing his finger at you accusingly, your best defense against attack is the integrity of your life. Study Isaiah 54:17 and 18 in the *Amplified Version*.

2. The personal consecration of Paul and his team — the integrity they exhibited before others and how they never took advantage of people financially — was their best defense. Study the book of Proverbs, and take note of the character traits that consistently result in blessing and success.

Recommended Resources

They received the word with all readiness of mind,
and searched the scriptures daily.
— Acts 17:11

To extend your study on overcoming attacks and advancing beyond hindrances, visit **renner.org** to obtain these and other books by Rick Renner. Each one will deepen your understanding of how to utilize your spiritual equipment, strengthen your character, and collaborate with the ministry of the Holy Spirit so you can live habitually clothed in Christ and stay fully equipped for spiritual battle.

1. *Dressed To Kill: A Biblical Approach to Spiritual Warfare and Armor*
2. *Dream Thieves: Overcoming Obstacles To Fulfill Your Dreams*
3. *Ten Guidelines To Help You Achieve Your Long-Awaited Promotion!*
4. *You Can Get Over It*
5. *Just Say Yes*
6. *Life in the Combat Zone*
7. *Spiritual Weapons To Defeat the Enemy*
8. *Sparkling Gems 1*
9. *Sparkling Gems 2*
10. *The Holy Spirit and You*

OTHER BENEFICIAL STUDY AIDS

1. *How To Use New Testament Greek Study Aids* by Walter Jerry Clark
2. *Strong's Exhaustive Concordance of the Bible* by James H. Strong
3. *The Interlinear Greek-English New Testament* by George Ricker Berry
4. *The Englishman's Greek Concordance of the New Testament* by George Wigram
5. *Word Studies in the Greek New Testament* by Kenneth Wuest
6. *New Testament Words* by William Barclay
7. *The Expanded Vine's Expository Dictionary of New Testament Words* by W. E. Vine

A Prayer To Receive Salvation

If you've never received Jesus as your Savior and Lord, now is the time for you to experience the new life Jesus wants to give you! To receive God's gift of salvation that can be obtained through Jesus alone, pray this prayer from your heart:

> *Jesus, I repent of my sin and receive You as my Savior and Lord. Wash away my sin with Your precious blood and make me completely new. I thank You that my sin is removed, and Satan no longer has any right to lay claim on me. Through Your empowering grace, I faithfully promise that I will serve You as my Lord for the rest of my life.*

If you just prayed this prayer of salvation, you are born again! You are a brand-new creation in Christ! Would you please let us know of your decision by going to **renner.org/salvation**? We would love to connect with you and pray for you as you begin your new life in Christ.

Scriptures for further study: John 3:16; John 14:6; Acts 4:12; Ephesians 1:7; Hebrews 10:19,20; 1 Peter 1:18,19; Romans 10:9,10; Colossians 1:13; 2 Corinthians 5:17; Romans 6:4; 1 Peter 1:3

Notes

CLAIM YOUR FREE RESOURCE!

As a way of introducing you further to the teaching ministry of Rick Renner, we would like to send you FREE of charge his teaching, "How To Receive a Miraculous Touch From God" on CD or as an MP3 download.

In His earthly ministry, Jesus commonly healed *all* who were sick of *all* their diseases. In this profound message, learn about the manifold dimensions of Christ's wisdom, goodness, power, and love toward all humanity who came to Him in faith with their needs.

☑ YES, I want to receive Rick Renner's monthly teaching letter!

Simply scan the QR code to claim this resource or go to: **renner.org/claim-your-free-offer**

Connect

WITH US!

www.ingramcontent.com/pod-product-compliance
Lightning Source LLC
Chambersburg PA
CBHW071458070426
42452CB00040B/1881